WHO
AM I?

WHO AM I?

Test Your Biography IQ

Based on the Biography Magazine
Column by Kurt Rieschick

Gramercy Books
New York

This 2000 edition is published by Gramercy Books™,
an imprint of Random House Value Publishing, Inc.,
280 Park Avenue, New York, New York 10017,
by arrangement with Andrews McMeel Publishing.

Gramercy Books™ and design are trademarks of
Random House Value Publishing, Inc.

Random House
New York • Toronto • London • Sydney • Auckland
http://www.randomhouse.com/

Printed and bound in the United States of America

A CIP catalog record for this book is available
from the Library of Congress.

ISBN 0-517-16227-X

8 7 6 5 4 3 2 1

To the memory of Kurt Rieschick,
who took such pleasure in writing *Who Am I?*
and whose good humor
and friendship is greatly missed.

FOREWORD

One of the most popular features in *Biography Magazine* is our monthly *Who Am I?* quiz, which challenges readers to identify famous people based on brief, first-person descriptions. The mystery subjects can date back to before the time of Christ—or be as current as this year's Oscar winner. They're men and women, heroes and villains, artists, scientists, performers, explorers, presidents, and politicians—to name just a few categories. But they're all familiar names—even though it may take some puzzle solving to come up with them.

Now we're pleased to present a collection of 150 of our best *Who Am I?* questions composed by the column's originator, Kurt Rieschick. We invite you to challenge your memory, test your *Biography* IQ, and see how many of these famous folks *you* can identify.

—Paulette McLeod
Publisher and Editor-in-Chief
Biography Magazine

The answer for each trivia question may be found on the page following the question.

1 **I was born in Ulm, Germany, in 1879 and won the Nobel Prize for physics in 1921.** I was able to prove that the inertia of a body depends on its energy content, as well as the theory that both time and motion are relative. I died in 1955 after a lifetime of helping mankind understand more about the structure of the universe than any scientist since Isaac Newton.

2 **At the age of twenty, I inherited patent rights to an oil tool drill; manufacturing the drill gave me my start.** I eventually created a financial empire, becoming a billionaire through my interests in aircraft manufacturing, movie production, real-estate development, and hotel ownership. I produced films, including *Hell's Angels* (1930) and *The Front Page* (1931). I gained control of RKO Studios and Trans World Airlines, and owned several famous hotels in Las Vegas. I died an eccentric recluse in 1976.

3 I became the best-known atheist in America when, in 1959, I filed a lawsuit on behalf of my son, arguing that a public school day should not begin with prayer. The Supreme Court agreed in 1963. In the mid '60s, my *American Atheist* radio series was broadcast on some four thousand radio stations, and I had more than twenty-five books published on the subject of atheism, including *Why I Am an Atheist* (1965).

Who Am I?

4 My name is Mrs. Charles A. Black. I'm a wife and mother, and have carved out a career in public service—as a member of the U.S. delegation to the United Nations General Assembly, as White House chief of protocol in 1976 and 1977, and as ambassador both to Ghana and to Czechoslovakia. However, I am best remembered as the most popular child actor of all time. I was a movie star at the age of five, leading box-office moneymaker at seven, and retired from the big screen at age twenty-one.

Who Am I?

5 *TV Guide* has ranked me the fiftieth greatest TV star of all time because of the success of my variety shows from 1948 until my retirement from TV in 1971. I first gained prominence in 1932 for my column, "Little Old New York," published in the New York *Daily News* and syndicated nationally. My expressionless manner and my promise to the audience every week that they could expect "a really big show" made me a television institution.

6 I was awarded the Pulitzer Prize for poetry four times, and was one of the most popular American poets of the twentieth century. After living in England for a few years (1912–14), I moved back to the United States and settled in New Hampshire, where I wrote about the people and landscape of New England. President John F. Kennedy asked me to recite a poem at his inauguration. I died at the age of eighty-nine in 1963.

Who Am I?

7

On January 22, 1997, I made history by being confirmed unanimously as secretary of state, the highest U.S. government post ever held by a woman. Born in Czechoslovakia in 1937, I came to America when I was eleven. I served as an adviser on foreign policy during the presidential campaigns of Walter Mondale, Michael Dukakis, and Bill Clinton. For four years, I was the U.S. permanent representative to the United Nations.

8 **A well-respected Indianapolis preacher during the 1950s, I formed the People's Temple and moved to California and then Guyana with a thousand of my followers.** When Congressman Leo J. Ryan attempted to leave Guyana after an investigation of my compound, I ordered him killed. The following day, I orchestrated the suicide of 912 men, women, and children, who drank cyanide-laced punch. I was found with my followers, a bullet in my head.

9

9 My maiden name was Mary Martha Corinne Boggs. Both my parents were Democratic members of Congress from Louisiana. My father, Hale, was House majority leader. I have been a reporter for National Public Radio, a political correspondent for ABC-TV's *World News Tonight,* and a regular panelist on *This Week with David Brinkley.* After Brinkley retired, I became the show's cohost with Sam Donaldson.

Q. 8 Jim Jones

10 **At twelve, I took voice lessons in hopes of becoming an opera singer, but I eventually developed an interest in acting.** I majored in drama at Vassar College, and did my graduate work at the Yale School of Drama. For the past twenty years, I have been considered one of the most talented leading ladies of the American stage and screen. I am well known for my ability to mimic accents. Some of my most memorable performances can be seen in the movies *Kramer vs. Kramer, Sophie's Choice, Silkwood,* and *Out of Africa.*

11

My father, Eugene Meyer, bought the financially ailing *Washington Post* newspaper in 1933. My husband, Philip, became publisher in 1946, a position he held until his suicide in 1963. At that time, even though I was raising four children, I took over the paper's helm, becoming the first woman to head a Fortune 500 company, and also assumed the responsibility for *Newsweek* magazine and our television and radio enterprises. Today, the *Washington Post* is one of the most highly respected newspapers in the world. Early in 1997, my best-selling autobiography, *Personal History*, was published.

12 Although I lived only forty-four years, I am considered one of the great American writers of the twentieth century and the literary spokesman for the "Jazz Age." I lived my celebrated life in New York City and on the French Riviera. My later years were marred by financial worries and the insanity of my wife, Zelda. My works include *This Side of Paradise*, *The Beautiful and the Damned*, and my most famous story, *The Great Gatsby*.

13 If jazz is America's classical music, I became America's greatest classical composer, publishing over nine hundred compositions ranging from popular songs to symphonic and religious pieces. I won nationwide attention in the 1920s through my radio broadcasts from Harlem's Cotton Club, with songs such as "Sophisticated Lady" and "It Don't Mean a Thing If It Ain't Got That Swing."

14

My nickname is "the Big O." After playing for the University of Cincinnati, I became one of professional basketball's greatest players with the Cincinnati Royals and Milwaukee Bucks. Even though I'm relatively short at 6' 4", I averaged a triple-double (a game in which I made at least 10 points, 10 assists, and 10 rebounds) in every game for my first five years in the NBA, an extraordinary accomplishment in basketball even now. I achieved a record 9,887 lifetime assists and 26,710 points, fifth on the all-time scoring list.

Who Am I?

Who Am I?

15

I was born in 1937, the son of Jamaican immigrants. Joining the army in the 1950s, I served two tours in Vietnam, was an adviser to Caspar Weinberger at the Defense Department, became national security adviser after the "Irangate" scandal, and, in 1989, was made a four-star general and chairman of the Joint Chiefs of Staff. My last and perhaps most important task was the overall administration of the allied forces in Saudi Arabia during the Gulf War in 1991.

16 I was born Agnes Gonxha Bojaxhiu in 1910 and was honored with the Nobel Peace Prize in 1979. I founded the Missionaries of Charity in India in 1950, and, together with my followers, helped lepers, the disabled, and the poor throughout the world.

17

Through my efforts, California migrant farm workers received health benefits, the right to collective bargaining, and, between 1964 and 1980, a 70-percent increase in wages. As founder and president of the United Farm Workers Union, I adopted a strategy of economic boycotts to keep the plight of migrant workers in the public eye.

Who Am I?

18

As an electrician at the Lenin Shipyard in Gdansk, Poland, I became a trade-union organizer. I founded the independent trade union Solidarity in 1980, and led a series of strikes that drew wide public support. In 1983, I was awarded the Nobel Peace Prize, and was elected president of Poland in December 1990.

19

When I was twenty years old, I became king of Macedonia, and by thirty had conquered nearly all the known world from the Danube River to India. I was a pupil of Aristotle and spread his teachings throughout my kingdom. Even though I was only thirty-two years old when I died in 323 B.C., I am considered one of the greatest military leaders who ever lived.

20

I head one of the largest privately owned companies in the United States today, partly because of such tongue-in-cheek advertising as "My chickens eat better than you do."

My experience with poultry started in the 1920s when, as a child, I was given fifty chicks to tend on the family farm. By 1994, my company operated ten processing plants in six states, ringing up $1.3 billion in sales.

21 I was born on August 9, 1957, in New York City. My mother is actress Tippi Hedren. I've been in numerous movies since my debut in *The Drowning Pool* in 1975, and received an Oscar nomination for my performance in *Working Girl.* In 1996, I married actor Antonio Banderas, my costar in the movie *Two Much,* and gave birth to a baby daughter. I was also married to Don Johnson twice, in 1975 and again in 1989.

22

I am a superstar in my sport—stock-car racing. Since my career began in 1975, my black No. 3 Chevrolet and I have won more money than any car and driver in auto-racing history, totaling almost $26 million. By 1998 I had won seventy races and was NASCAR champion seven times.

23

Who Am I?

Time magazine wasn't wrong when in 1974 it chose me as one of America's two hundred "Faces of the Future." I served under every president from Lyndon Johnson to George Bush. From 1983 to 1987, I was secretary of transportation, and in 1989 and 1990, secretary of labor. In 1991, I became president of the American Red Cross, later taking a leave of absence to help my husband.

24 I was born in Tuskegee, Alabama, in 1913. On December 1, 1955, when coming home from my job as a seamstress in a department store, I refused to give up my seat to a white man on a Montgomery, Alabama, bus. My arrest and jailing led to a 381-day bus boycott led by Dr. Martin Luther King Jr., and inspired civil-rights activities around the country.

25

Although I was a child of the backwoods, orphaned at fourteen, I became the seventh president of the United States, serving two terms, from 1829 to 1837. Prior to politics, I had a long, distinguished military career. I became the one great hero of the War of 1812 when I defended New Orleans against seasoned British troops. After serving as president, I retired to my home, called the Hermitage, and lived out my life despised by my enemies and revered as "Old Hickory" by my supporters.

26 I am perhaps the most popular and powerful woman in the history of motion pictures. I was able to control my films, both creatively and commercially, becoming famous worldwide. I convincingly played children's roles well into my thirties. Some of my films include *Poor Little Rich Girl* (1917), *Rebecca of Sunnybrook Farm* (1917), *Pollyanna* (1920), and *Sparrows* (1926). I won an Oscar for my first talkie, *Coquette*, in 1929. That same year, I made *The Taming of the Shrew* with my husband, actor Douglas Fairbanks.

Who Am I?

27

As a freshman senator, I broke with my Republican colleagues by voting for Richard Nixon's impeachment. I also voiced my doubts about White House involvement during the Iran-Contra hearings. Even though I am a Republican, President Clinton chose me to be his secretary of defense, replacing William Perry.

Q.26 Mary Pickford

28

President Ulysses S. Grant and his entire cabinet followed my bier up Broadway in New York City before I was laid to rest at Woodlawn Cemetery in the Bronx in 1870. I became America's first naval officer to achieve the rank of admiral. My most famous victory took place on August 5, 1864, during the Civil War. At that time, I defeated the Confederate flotilla at Mobile Bay, exclaiming, "Damn the torpedoes! Full speed ahead!"

Who Am I?

29

I was a French author. I lived to be seventy-four years old, but spent twenty-seven of those years in prisons and asylums, mainly because of my theory that sexual deviation and criminal acts are natural to human beings. I wrote plays and novels dealing explicitly with a variety of sexual practices. My most famous novel, *Justine*, was published in 1791 and remains popular today.

Who Am I?

30

I am an American writer and humorist. My hometown of Anoka, Minnesota, inspired my stories about Lake Wobegon, "the town that time forgot, that decades cannot improve." I have written nine books, among them *Lake Wobegon Days* and most recently *Wobegon Boy*. I am probably best known for my weekly radio monologues on the NPR show, *A Prairie Home Companion*.

31

I was born in Boston, Massachusetts, in 1706 and, during my eighty-four years authored *Poor Richard's Almanack*, helped to draft the Declaration of Independence, achieved the repeal of the Stamp Act, and, as ambassador to France, was one of the signatories to the Treaty of Versailles in 1783, by which independence was secured for the United States.

32

In 1953, I was named Television Man of the Year. I received one of the first Emmy awards, that of Most Outstanding Personality. My show, *Life Is Worth Living,* was one of the most popular on television—an unusual occurrence because it was a religious program and I, the host, a Roman Catholic clergyman!

33 I was the first woman pilot to make a solo transatlantic flight, in 1932, and the first person to fly solo from Hawaii to California, in 1935. In 1937, I set out to fly around the world. I was lost when my plane mysteriously disappeared over the Pacific.

Q.32 Bishop Fulton J. Sheen

34

In 1989 Iran's late Ayatollah Khomeini declared my 1988 book, *The Satanic Verses,* blasphemous. He ordered me, and anyone connected with the book, killed under a religious edict called a *fatwa,* and I went into hiding. In 1998, the *fatwa* was officially lifted, making me a free man. Unfortunately, a militant Muslim religious foundation increased the price on my head, and presumably its followers are in search of me.

35 As queen of England, I became one of the most venerated monarchs in history. **I ruled from 1837 until my death in 1901, during which time I married my first cousin, Albert, and had nine children. Their marriages, and those of my grandchildren, allied the British royal house with those of Russia, Germany, Greece, Denmark, and Romania.**

36

Michael Jordan has said that his only real hero on earth is me. By age five, I had already appeared on *The Mike Douglas Show* and *That's Incredible!* What's really incredible is that even before I played in my first professional tournament, I had signed endorsement contracts for more than $60 million. I was named *Sports Illustrated*'s Sportsman of the Year for 1996.

37

My family fled Havana, Cuba, in 1959 when I was two years old, and settled in Miami, Florida. I have been a top female recording artist for the past decade, writing music and lyrics to most of my hit singles. I wrote and sang the Olympic anthem "Reach," which was inspired by my recovery from a 1990 bus accident in which I was severely injured while on tour.

38

A humorist and political satirist, I was a popular radio and press personality, and with the advent of sound in motion pictures, became a box-office attraction as well. **I turned down the nomination for the governorship of Oklahoma, but did serve as mayor of Beverly Hills. I died in a plane crash along with aviator Wiley Post in 1935.**

39

I was a fighter pilot during World War II, and became a test pilot during the early postwar years. In 1947, I became the first person to fly faster than the speed of sound. In 1953, I also set a world speed record, reaching 1,650 mph. I wrote my autobiography in 1985, and have since appeared on numerous television shows and in commercials. I still fly planes as a test pilot, although I'm seventy-six years old.

Who Am I ?

A. 39 Will Rogers

40

My nickname is "the Great One." I led the Edmonton Oilers of the National Hockey League to four Stanley Cup championships. I also led the league nine times in scoring, and was named its most valuable player nine times. I am the all-time points leader for goals and assists. In 1994, I surpassed Gordie Howe by setting a new record for the most career goals in the history of the NHL.

41 After my company went bankrupt, I moved to California in 1923 and, with Ub Iwerks and my older brother, Roy, began producing a series of animated cartoons. My first cartoon with sound was *Steamboat Willie,* for which I provided the star's characteristic high-pitched voice. During my career, I collected twenty-nine Academy Awards for my films. I died in 1966 and am still America's undisputed king of family entertainment.

42

Saturday Night Live periodically satirized my TV cooking show, *The French Chef.* I studied at the famed Cordon Bleu in Paris. In 1951, with two French women, I founded a cooking school, L'École des Trois Gourmandes. In 1961, I wrote the best-selling cookbook *Mastering the Art of French Cooking.*

43

I have been able to turn my own lifestyle into a mega-industry. I was a successful model during the late 1950s and early 1960s, and an even more successful Wall Street stockbroker until I launched a catering business that grew into a million-dollar-a-year operation. In 1982, I wrote a best-selling book, *Entertaining*. My ideas about gracious living, coupled with business acumen, have made me a fortune.

44

I opened a five-and-ten-cent store in Lancaster, Pennsylvania, in 1879; within twenty-one years I owned over one thousand such establishments. In 1913, I built the world's then-tallest building in New York City, but died six years later of septic poisoning when I refused to see a dentist.

Who Am I?

45

I spent $30 million for a Leonardo da Vinci notebook at a Christie's auction, and $50 million for my new home. **However, I still fly coach class on planes because I don't need the wider seats of first class. In 1998, my net worth was estimated at $58.4 billion, the highest in the world. I wonder what I could have accomplished had I not dropped out of Harvard.**

Q.44 Frank Winfield Woolworth

46 **I was born in 1869 in Porbandar, India. I studied law in London and settled in South Africa, where I led my countrymen in opposition to racial discrimination.** Upon returning to my homeland, I led the struggle for Indian independence from Great Britain by advocating nonviolent noncooperation. I was assassinated in 1948 by a Hindu nationalist.

47

As one of America's greatest authors, I achieved a high degree of literary celebrity during my lifetime. My 1952 novella, *The Old Man and the Sea,* won the Pulitzer Prize for fiction in 1953, and I received the Nobel Prize for literature in 1954. Some of my outstanding works include *The Sun Also Rises, A Farewell to Arms,* and *For Whom the Bell Tolls.* Still, despite my fame, plagued by deep depression and ill health, I committed suicide on July 2, 1961.

48

I was the first Englishman to circumnavigate the globe, on the ship *Golden Hind*. Along the way I robbed Spanish ships and raided Spanish settlements. I was knighted by Queen Elizabeth I, and was an admiral in the fleet that defeated the Spanish Armada. My last expedition ended in Panama, where I died of dysentery in 1596.

49

In 1155, I became chancellor of England, and in 1162 I was elected and consecrated as Archbishop of Canterbury, the highest church office in England. Unable to reach a compromise with Henry II over the coronation ceremony of his son Henry the Younger in 1170, I was brutally murdered by agents of the king. I was canonized in 1173. Richard Burton and Peter O'Toole starred in a 1964 movie about me that earned several Oscar nominations.

50 **Born in 1755 in Rhode Island, I was a student of Benjamin West for six years in England, studying portraiture.** I returned to the United States and opened a successful studio in Philadelphia in 1794. Soon after, I completed two paintings of George Washington that now hang in the National Gallery in Washington, D.C., and the Pennsylvania Academy of the Fine Arts. However, my most famous work graces the front of the one-dollar bill.

51

My husband of seventeen years, Garry Trudeau, is the famous creator of *Doonesbury.* In October 1976, at the age of twenty-five, after four years as a cub reporter in my hometown of Indianapolis, I landed one of the most coveted and prestigious positions in television news, that of a regular member of the *Today* show. My maternity leave from the show in 1983 was one of the most widely publicized pregnancies in TV history. I had twins!

Who Am I?

52

Although I eventually committed suicide in 183 B.C. to avoid capture by the Romans, I will always be considered one of the great military leaders of all time. At age twenty-six, I became the Carthaginian commander in chief in Spain, where, during the Second Punic War, I set out to invade Italy by crossing the Pyrenees with a small force of hand-picked troops and thirty-eight war elephants. At Cannae in 216 B.C., I won one of the most brilliant victories in history.

53

I have the second most popular radio talk show in the United States today (after Rush Limbaugh), with more than twelve million daily listeners. I have written two best-selling books, *Ten Stupid Things Women Do to Mess Up Their Lives* and *How Could You Do That?! The Abdication of Character, Courage and Conscience.* I start each show by announcing that "I am my kid's mom," praise some callers, criticize others, and finally end my show by commanding my audience, "Now, go take on the day."

54 I have been a lawyer and a Democratic state legislator from Mississippi, and am now a professional writer. Industry analysts have ranked me with such perennial best-selling authors as Stephen King, Danielle Steel, and Michael Crichton. Over the past ten years, my nine novels have allowed me, my wife, and our two children to live comfortably in our two homes, one in Mississippi, the other in Virginia.

55

I became ruler of the Roman Empire in A.D. 54 when my mother, Agrippina, murdered my stepfather, Claudius. I was popular early in my reign, but my support dwindled after I imposed heavy taxes to rebuild Rome after a fire destroyed it. In A.D. 68 I fled my palace and was declared a public enemy by the senate. When caught, after being threatened with an "ancient style" punishment (flogging and death), I committed suicide by stabbing myself in the throat with a dagger. My death ended the Caesarean line.

56

I was born in 1853 at Zundert, Holland, and died thirty-seven years later from a self-inflicted gunshot wound. My eleven years as an artist were marred by insanity and the cutting off of part of my right ear. Most of my paintings, including *The Sunflowers, Memories of the North,* and *The Rising of Lazarus,* were produced in a twenty-nine-month period of frenzied activity.

Who Am I?

57

President Ronald Reagan appointed me surgeon general in 1981. I received a great deal of media attention because of my forceful statements on the dangers of both AIDS and smoking. As head of the U.S. Public Health Service, it was my responsibility to protect the people's health, report on health issues, and collaborate with other countries on health-related subjects. In June 1997, I was influential in helping the government reach a settlement with the tobacco industry.

58. **I was born the son of a slave in 1856, and worked in salt furnaces and coal mines until I entered the Hampton Institute in Virginia, where, in 1879, I became an instructor and developed the first night school.** In 1881, I was chosen to organize Tuskegee Institute, which became a leading black educational institution. I had many published works, including my autobiography, *Up from Slavery* (1901).

59

"My mother thanks you, my father thanks you, my sister thanks you, and I thank you." With these words I ended each performance of our vaudeville act. President Franklin Roosevelt awarded me a special Congressional Medal of Honor for my song "You're a Grand Old Flag." During my funeral in 1942, the organ at Saint Patrick's played my composition "Over There," the first time a secular song had ever been played at the cathedral.

60

I was one of the most progressive Roman emperors.

During my reign, I instituted a centralized bureaucracy, separated military from civil government, and introduced many legal reforms. I am best remembered for accepting and promoting Christianity, and for transferring the capital of the empire from Rome to Byzantium.

Who Am I?

61 Unfortunately, I convinced Henry VIII to divorce his first wife, Catherine of Aragon, by promising him a male heir if he married me. After breaking with the pope and founding the Church of England, he married me in 1533. He had me beheaded three years later. I did, however, give birth to the future queen, Elizabeth I.

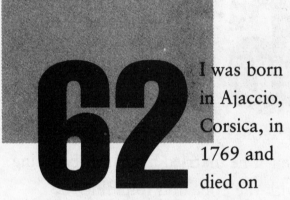

62 I was born in Ajaccio, Corsica, in 1769 and died on the island of St. Helena in 1821. **Through ambition, drive, and intelligence, I became emperor of France, conquered much of Europe, and forever changed the course of European history.**

63

During World War II, I did research on the atom bomb at Columbia University and was instrumental in the first successful hydrogen bomb explosion in 1952. From 1952 to 1960, I was the director of the Livermore Radiation Laboratory at the University of California, and later helped create the concept for Ronald Reagan's Strategic Defense Initiative, better known as "Star Wars."

Who Am I?

64

I was born in Philadelphia, Pennsylvania, in 1929 and became a major film star, winning the 1954 Academy Award for my performance in *The Country Girl.* My celebrated marriage in 1956 to the ruling prince of Monaco, Rainier III, drew worldwide attention. My life was cut short when I was killed in an automobile accident in 1982.

Who Am I?

65

Honored in America as a pioneering feminist, I edited *Revolution* from 1868 to 1870. This radical, crusading journal demanded woman suffrage and equal access to education and employment opportunities, and encouraged women to form trade unions. In May 1869, along with Elizabeth Cady Stanton, I formed the National Woman Suffrage Association. I've been honored by having my face appear on the American silver dollar.

66 My father, Junius Brutus, came from England to the United States in 1821 and became the foremost tragic actor of his day. My brother Edwin became a famous Shakespearean actor, as did I. His hundred-night run of *Hamlet* in New York City in 1864 won him wide acclaim. The next year, he retired briefly from the stage because of the historic crime in which I was involved. I died from a gunshot wound shortly after my deed, but it is not known whether it was by my own hand or by that of another.

Who Am I?

67

I was fortunate to be born both beautiful and rich (my grandfather was F. W. Woolworth). My luck failed to hold, though, through seven marriages, all unhappy. I called my grandfather's mausoleum "The Pyramid," and joined him there when I died in 1979.

68

I became the first black woman to win the Miss America pageant, a position from which I subsequently resigned after erotic photos of me were published in *Penthouse* magazine. Since that time, I have released five albums, one of which, *The Comfort Zone*, went double platinum in 1992.

Who Am I?

69

Before I married the man who would become the thirty-eighth president of the United States, I pursued a number of careers. I was a teenage model at a store in Grand Rapids, Michigan, and was later a dance student. After college and a stint with the Martha Graham dance troupe in New York, I became a fashion coordinator and a volunteer teacher of dance for handicapped children. As first lady, my candor about my mastectomy was credited with inspiring thousands of women to seek medical advice for symptoms of breast cancer.

Q. 68 Vanessa Williams

70 I became *Time* magazine's Man of the Decade for the 1980s mainly because, as the head of the Soviet Union, I initiated a policy of restructuring, known as *perestroika,* and introduced a climate of openness, called *glasnost.* In 1987, I visited the United States, where I signed the historic Intermediate-Range Nuclear Forces Treaty with President Reagan.

71

I denounced my fellow evangelist, Jim Bakker, when a sex scandal rocked his ministry in 1987. Unfortunately for me, I, too, was forced to humble myself in a tearful confession in front of television cameras after church officials were shown photographs of me visiting a prostitute.

72

Even though I am over eighty years old, I still work as a news commentator, reaching over twelve million listeners daily. My broadcasts have been heard across the nation since 1951. In addition to my radio work, I write syndicated newspaper columns and maintain a busy speaking schedule. Each edition of my show opens with the greeting, "Hello, Americans. Stand by . . . for news!" and ends with my signature, "G'day!"

Who Am I?

73

I am considered one of the most brilliant theoretical physicists of our time. My key areas of study are the astronomical bodies known as black holes and research that supports the big bang theory. In 1988 I wrote a best-selling book, *A Brief History of Time*. Because of a muscle disease, I can barely move or speak and must use a wheelchair.

74 I was chairman of the Joint Chiefs of Staff from 1949 to 1953. During World War II, I led the Second U.S. Army Corps to its victories in Tunisia and Sicily, which caused the surrender of 250,000 Axis troops. In 1944, I led the U.S. troops in the invasion of France. My Twelfth Army regiment grew to 1.3 million troops, the largest U.S. force ever assembled.

Who Am I?

75

I was the founder of psychoanalysis. Early in my career, I collaborated with Josef Breuer on the use of hypnosis in the treatment of hysteria. After rejecting this concept, I devised the technique of free association, emphasizing infantile sexuality and the Oedipus complex. With the Nazi occupation of Austria in 1938, I fled to England, where I died a year later.

76

I was born Israel Baline in Russia in 1888, but by five years of age I was singing for pennies on New York's Lower East Side. I began writing songs as a teenager. My first big hit was "Alexander's Ragtime Band," published in 1911. Although I could play and compose only in the key of F sharp, I became one of America's most celebrated composers. My most famous song is probably "White Christmas."

77

After teaching in elementary school for two years, I turned my attention to my first love, singing.

My first professional role came in 1961, playing Rodolfo in *La Bohème*. Seven years later, playing the same role, I made my debut at New York's Metropolitan Opera. I am one of the rare singers capable of reaching a high C. I have been the world's most famous operatic tenor for the past thirty years.

78

I was born in 469 B.C. in Athens, Greece, and am one of the most colorful figures in the history of philosophy. **My major contributions lay in leading individuals to an awareness of their own ignorance so they could discover the truth. Plato, my most famous student, was with me when I was forced to commit suicide by drinking a cup of poisonous hemlock.**

79

I was the grandson of one of the richest men in the United States. A liberal Republican, I served as governor of New York from 1959 through 1973. I unsuccessfully sought the presidential nomination three times during the 1960s, but was named vice president under the Twenty-fifth Amendment of the Constitution. My collection of primitive art was world renowned.

WHO AM I?

80 In 1969, I was a star quarterback at the University of Alabama and became the highest-paid rookie in professional football history, signing a $400,000 contract. I orchestrated the stunning victory of my team, the New York Jets, over the Baltimore Colts in the Super Bowl. I believe I am also the only quarterback in history to appear in a TV commercial wearing a pair of panty hose.

81 Many consider me the greatest scientist of all time. I was born in England in 1642 and became a mathematician and physicist. Among my many achievements were discovering the law of universal gravitation, building the first reflecting telescope, and discovering that white light is composed of every color in the spectrum. I was president of the Royal Society from 1703 until my death in 1727.

82

The artistic director of the Royal National Theatre in London has called me the best actor of my generation, but in America I am best known as the man on the Infiniti automobile commercials. I won a Tony award for my role in the 1976 production of *Comedians,* was the original Engineer in the London production of *Miss Saigon,* and was the 1995 Cannes Film Festival's choice for best actor for *Carrington.* After Americans see me in more mainstream movies, from *Evita* to *Ronin,* I hope I'll be recognized as more than just a car salesman.

83 I was a professor of astronomy and space sciences at Cornell University, and won a Pulitzer Prize in 1977 for my book *The Dragons of Eden.* I was able to reach an international audience of 400 million with my 1980 PBS series, *Cosmos.*

84

"It's hard for somebody to hit you when you've got your fist in their face" was my basic philosophy during the 1992 presidential campaign, in which I helped Bill Clinton through a bruising primary and then on to victory over George Bush. **In 1993, I married my counterpart in the '92 Republican presidential race, Mary Matalin, and in July of 1995 became the father of a baby girl. The following year my book, *We're Right, They're Wrong,* became a handbook for political progressives.**

Who Am I ?

85

Born in 1758, I became one of England's greatest naval heroes during the French Revolutionary Wars, when I defeated the French fleet at Abukir, crippling Napoleon's Egyptian expedition. In 1801, I defeated the Danes at Copenhagen. But my greatest victory was against the combined fleets of France and Spain at Trafalgar. I was mortally wounded during the battle.

86

To many, I am the most powerful person in the United States (after the president) because, as chairman of the Federal Reserve Board, I control our nation's money supply. A few words of concern from me about an increase in inflation can, and usually does, send the stock market into a tailspin. I was easily confirmed by the Senate, and took office on August 11, 1987. I am a moderate Republican who believes the fight against inflation to be the board's principal duty.

A.85 Horatio Nelson

WHO AM I?

87

After consolidating my own kingdom, I invaded Italy in support of the pope and, in A.D. 774, was crowned king of the Lombards. In 800, I restored Leo III to the papacy, and he crowned me emperor on Christmas Day, laying the foundation for the Holy Roman Empire. I ruled through a highly efficient administrative system and enforced a code of laws throughout the lands of my dominion. My court at Aachen was the center of an intellectual and artistic renaissance.

88 I was appointed to Al Gore's Senate seat when he became vice president in 1993. Even though I have appeared in many movies, my most important role has been chairing the hearings on illegal foreign donations and other fund-raising abuses that allegedly occurred during the 1996 presidential campaign. Perhaps I was chosen for this task because of my experience on the Senate Watergate committee, when I asked the question, "Were President Nixon's conversations taped?"

89

I was born in Braunas, Austria, in 1889, and served in the Bavarian Army during World War I. I was gassed and wounded, and I received the Iron Cross for bravery. In 1920, I became the founder and leader of National Socialism. Three years later, I attempted the overthrow of my government in what became known as the "Beer Hall Putsch." My nine months' imprisonment was well spent, allowing me time to write a book that enhanced my reputation throughout the nation.

90

I am a successful writer who was born in New Orleans, Louisiana. My obsession with the supernatural is evident in my novels, including *Interview with the Vampire, The Vampire Lestat,* and *The Witching Hour.* In the mid-1980s, under the name A. N. Roquelaure, I wrote three novels dealing with hardcore sadomasochism. I have been married for more than thirty years and consider myself a totally conservative person.

Who Am I?

91

My last name is Galilei, but the world knows me by my first name. I was born in Pisa, Italy, in 1564. My inventions included the telescope, and my observations led me to believe that the earth orbited the sun. I was unable to publish my findings for fear of punishment by the Catholic Church during the Inquisition.

92 After defeating Pompey in a civil war, I became dictator of Rome. I was a general, statesman, orator, and historian, and was one of the greatest leaders of the Roman republic. I wrote vivid accounts of my conquest of Gaul that are still read today. I was murdered by Brutus and other conspirators in 44 B.C.

93

I may be the only millionaire who started out selling paper cups. For nearly twenty years I was a salesman for the Lily cup company, eventually moving on to multiple-milkshake mixers. In 1955, my concept of combining fast service and disposable eating utensils with consistent recipes and low prices led to the creation of the most famous of all franchise operations, McDonald's. Today, my fast-food restaurants employ 183,000 men and women and earn over $8.3 billion in annual sales.

94 As the founder of Bolshevism, I was a major force behind the founding of the Soviet Union. When the Russian Revolution broke out in 1917, I returned to Petrograd from my exile in Western Europe, and led the overthrow of the provisional government. I died in 1924. I'm considered one of the greatest and most practical revolutionaries of all time.

95

I received unprecedented acclaim when I astounded the world on May 21, 1927, by landing in Paris after a solo flight from New York. After my young son's death, my wife and I moved to England for several years; speeches I gave advocating United States neutrality in the worsening European political situation branded me pro-Nazi.

Who Am I?

96

I spent my youth observing life on the Mississippi River. During my seventy-five years, I was a printer, river steamboat pilot, newspaper correspondent, lecturer, and novelist. My most famous works are *The Adventures of Tom Sawyer, The Prince and the Pauper, A Connecticut Yankee in King Arthur's Court,* and *The Adventures of Huckleberry Finn.*

Who Am I?

97 At my funeral in 1799, the famous phrase "First in war, first in peace, and first in the hearts of his countrymen" was delivered by Robert E. Lee's father. While I was still commander in chief of the army, and prior to my presidential inauguration in New York City, a kidnap attempt resulted in the execution of my bodyguard for mutiny, sedition, and treachery. I was one of America's richest presidents, owning more than 33,000 acres of land, mostly in Virginia, where I was born. I am the only president who did not live in Washington, D.C.

98

I gained fame as a lawyer by defending the rights of the poor and abused of Cuba, many of whom could not pay my fee. In my struggle to overthrow the corrupt military dictatorship of Fulgencio Batista, I fought on the front lines with my band of revolutionary guerrillas. After the success of the campaign in 1959, I was honored with a ticker-tape parade in New York City. I am reviled by many, but to others I remain a symbol of revolution and social change in Latin America.

99

I was a French oceanographer and naval officer. In 1943, along with Emil Gagnan, I invented the Aqua-Lung. I founded the French navy's undersea research group in 1945, and in 1957 was made director of the oceanographic museum of Monaco. However, I was best known for documentary films aboard my ship, *Calypso,* and my half-dozen books, including *Life and Death in a Coral Sea* and *The Whale.* I died in June 1997.

100

I was recently named president of the National Rifle Association, but most of my adult life has been spent as a movie star. My Hollywood film debut occurred in 1950, and since then I have starred in more than fifty films, often playing larger-than-life characters. I won an Academy Award for the title role in 1959's *Ben-Hur*.

101

I was born in Tulsa, Oklahoma, in 1962. While I waited for my "big break" as a singer, I worked as a clerk in a Nashville, Tennessee, boot shop. Capitol Records signed me within six months of my arrival in Nashville, and "The Dance," the hit song from my first album in 1989, established me as the country music superstar of the 1990s. In 1992, my success exploded with the release of my fourth album, *The Chase,* which was number one on both the pop and country charts in its first week—a feat never before accomplished by a country-music performer. At the Twenty-third American Music Awards, I refused the favorite artist award because I didn't feel I deserved it.

102

The rock group I helped form rose to prominence in the mid-1960s and continues to exert great influence today. Brian Jones, Keith Richards, Ron Wood, Bill Wyman, Charlie Watts, and I appeared in concerts throughout the world, singing a variety of blues-inspired rock songs, including "Satisfaction," "Sympathy for the Devil," and "Paint It Black," which are some of our most popular.

103

By the time I was six days old, I had become queen of Scotland. At nineteen, I had already been married and widowed. In order to succeed Elizabeth I on the English throne, I married my English cousin, Lord Darnley. Two years later, he was mysteriously murdered. My lover, the Earl of Bothwell, was accused of the murder but acquitted. After several ill-fated plots against Elizabeth, I was brought to trial, found guilty of treason, and beheaded on February 8, 1587.

A. 102 Mick Jagger

104

An African-American woman lawyer, I was a public official and educator. As a Democratic member of the U.S. House of Representatives from 1973 to 1979, I achieved national renown as a member of the House Judiciary Committee when it investigated the Watergate affair in 1974.

105

After serving in the United States Coast Guard for twenty years, I moved to New York to pursue a writing career. In 1965, I collaborated with Malcolm X to write his autobiography. Although the book received praise from critics and was widely read in colleges, it wasn't until 1976 that my best-known work, *Roots: The Saga of an American Family,* hurtled me to the top of the best-seller lists. I received special citations from the Pulitzer Prize and National Book Award committees. *Roots* was translated into twenty-six languages, and the miniseries was one of the most-watched shows of all time.

106

I was born in 1874 at Blenheim Palace, England. During my career, I was a war correspondent, member of parliament, first lord of the admiralty, secretary of war, and prime minister. During my tenure as prime minister, I traveled to Washington, Casablanca, Cairo, Yalta, Quebec, and Tehran, meeting other leaders of the Allied war effort during World War II. I'm best known for my skill as an orator, and was the author of several historical books.

Who Am I?

107 In the fall of 1996, I was a consulting physician for Boris Yeltsin because of his heart problem. My reputation as a heart surgeon, however, began in 1963, when I developed a highly successful Dacron graft. In 1965, I headed a twenty-eight-member commission, established by President Lyndon Johnson, which proposed the establishment of regional centers for the care and study of heart disease. In 1966, I implanted the first completely artificial heart in a human patient.

108

Although born in south London, I became one of America's most famous movie stars. I was considered a comic genius, and was well loved as the "Little Tramp." Along with Mary Pickford, Douglas Fairbanks, and D. W. Griffith, I formed the United Artists film studios in 1919. When accused of Communist sympathies, I moved to Switzerland. Some of my best-remembered films are *City Lights, The Gold Rush,* and *The Great Dictator.*

109 Born of Portuguese nobility, I'm credited with proving the earth is round by being the first person to circumnavigate the globe. In reality I never achieved this goal, because I was killed by natives when I reached the Philippines. My voyage, backed by Charles I of Spain after my native country rejected my theories, began in 1519.

110

I was a French Protestant theologian, organist, and missionary surgeon. In 1913, I founded the hospital at Lambaréné in Gabon, Africa, giving organ recitals to support my work. My biography of Bach (1905), along with my renditions of Bach's organ music, made me one of the preeminent authorities on the composer. I won the Nobel Peace Prize in 1952 for my teaching about "reverence for life."

111

Twenty-eight years after my graduation from West Point, I became the supreme commander of the Allied Expeditionary Force. As the thirty-fourth president of the United States, I signed significant civil-rights legislation and sent federal troops to enforce school desegregation in Little Rock, Arkansas. I am probably the only president to have shot a hole in one in golf.

Who Am I ?

A: 110 Albert Schweitzer

112 I was born in Austria in 1756 and became a child prodigy, composing by the age of five. When I was six years old, I began performing concerts throughout Europe. I was arguably the greatest composer of all time, creating such famous works as *The Marriage of Figaro, Don Giovanni, The Magic Flute,* and *Requiem.* I died in poverty at age thirty-five and was buried in a pauper's grave.

113

I was the daughter of Chief Powhatan of the Powhatan Indians of Virginia, and reportedly saved the life of Captain John Smith. I was held hostage at Jamestown, Virginia, until my father freed captured English prisoners. I eventually became a Christian and, in 1614, married John Rolfe. During a visit to England in 1616, I was received as a princess. Unfortunately, I died before returning to America.

114

I was a general in the American Revolution and served with distinction in the assault on Quebec and the Battle of Saratoga. After these victories, I felt slighted and greatly resentful when I was not promoted. My plot with John André to betray the American post at West Point in 1780 was discovered, forcing me to flee the country. I later fought for the British, although they never trusted me. Who Am I?

115 I was the first African-American justice on the Supreme Court and am considered a pillar of the civil-rights movement. I won twenty-nine of the thirty-two cases I argued before the Supreme Court, including *Brown* v. *Board of Education,* which resulted in the outlawing of public school segregation in 1954. In the 1940s and 1950s, I traveled more than fifty thousand miles a year challenging local "Jim Crow" laws. After twenty-four years on the high court, I retired in 1991 and died two years later.

116

Although I lived a relatively short life (forty-two years), and ruled for only ten years (1189–99), I became a legendary hero. During my reign, I spent all but six months abroad. My fame was assured during the Third Crusade, when I won victories at Cyprus, Acre, and Messina against the great Saladin, but I was never able to recapture Jerusalem. While returning to England, I was captured by Leopold, Duke of Austria, and held prisoner until a huge ransom was paid.

117

I was born in Silver, South Carolina, in 1927. In 1948, I won the first of ten straight national Negro women's singles titles in tennis. I became the first African-American to play in the U.S. Nationals at Forest Hills in 1950, and at Wimbledon in 1951. In 1957, I captured both the singles and doubles titles at Wimbledon and the singles at Forest Hills. In 1958, I successfully defended all three titles. I also played professional golf!

Who Am I?

Q. 116 Richard the Lion-Hearted

118

I was a twenty-five-year-old reporter for Joseph Pulitzer when I set out to best the fictional Phileas Fogg's record trip around the world in eighty days. I completed my journey in seventy-two days, six hours, eleven minutes, and fourteen seconds, stopping in France along the way to interview Jules Verne, Fogg's creator. He wished me luck, but doubted that I could beat Fogg's time. I pioneered investigative journalism, exposing abuses in politics, hospitals, and prisons.

In 1896, I published a cookbook which became an instant success in homes across America, thanks to the standardized measurements I introduced for my recipes. I opened a cooking school, devised special diets for those recovering from illness, and even taught for a year at Harvard Medical School.

120

I was born John Chapman in Massachusetts in 1774 and was considered a true American pioneer. Dressed in rags, I wandered for forty years through Ohio, Indiana, and western Pennsylvania, sowing apple seeds. I am popularly known by what name?

121

I was born in Macedonia in 384 B.C. and developed the systematic discipline of logic.

Plato was my instructor, and Alexander the Great my student. Alexander spread my beliefs through his conquests. My logic was deeply flawed, however: I believed that almost everyone was innately inferior to Greek aristocratic men.

Who Am I?

122

I was one of the most colorful figures to emerge from the Watergate affair. As the Democratic senator from North Carolina, I was chairman of the Senate Select Committee to Investigate Presidential Campaign Practices during the nationally televised proceedings in 1973, and was credited with exemplifying the best in American politics for fairness, honesty, and a passion for truth.

123 I was considered one of the greatest and most versatile male athletes ever to compete in the United States. Part Native American, I played football at the Carlisle Indian School in Pennsylvania. In the 1912 Olympics, I won gold medals in both the pentathlon and decathlon, but was forced to surrender them when it was discovered that I had played semipro baseball.

124

I was the niece of the twenty-sixth president of the United States, married to the thirty-second president, and was influential in the social betterment of minorities and the poor. I was a lecturer, syndicated newspaper columnist, and world traveler. As a U.S. delegate to the United Nations, I was named chairman of the Commission for Human Rights in 1946. In the 1950s I became a leader of the liberal wing of the Democratic Party.

Who Am I?

125

In 1932 and 1933, I played on the University of Michigan's national championship football teams, and from 1935 to 1940 was the boxing coach and assistant varsity football coach at Yale. **I was elected to Congress in 1948 and served on the Warren Commission. I became House minority leader in 1965, a post I held until 1973, at which time I was confirmed as vice president under provisions of the Twenty-fifth Amendment. On August 9, 1974, I became the thirty-eighth president of the United States.**

Q. 124 Eleanor Roosevelt

126 I started in show business when I won a talent contest at a Greenwich Village bar. After my Broadway debut in *I Can Get It for You Wholesale,* my career skyrocketed. I won a best actress Oscar for my movie debut in *Funny Girl* in 1968, and another Oscar for best song for "Evergreen" in 1976. I have received two Emmy Awards and four Grammy Awards.

127 After escaping slavery in 1849, I became one of the most successful "conductors" on the Underground Railroad, leading more than three hundred slaves to freedom. During the Civil War, I was a friend of leading abolitionists, and worked as a laundress, nurse, and spy for the Union forces. According to the 1994 book *The Black 100,* by Columbus Salley, I am the most important black woman in American history.

128

Encouraged by Louis Leakey and funded by the National Geographic Society, I observed and studied the majestic, peaceable mountain gorillas for eighteen years in the Virunga Mountains of east-central Africa. In 1983, I wrote the book *Gorillas in the Mist*, which became a 1988 movie starring Sigourney Weaver. On December 26, 1985, my slain body was discovered in the forests of Rwanda near my home base, the Karisoke Research Center. It is suspected that I was the victim of poachers, whose decimation of the gorilla population I had long fought.

129 I won best actress Oscars for my performances in *Klute* in 1971 and *Coming Home* in 1978. I costarred with my famous father in the film *On Golden Pond.* I have been married three times: first to Roger Vadim, who directed me in the movie *Barbarella,* then to Tom Hayden during my anti-Vietnam and social activism days, and finally, since 1991, to Ted Turner, owner of the Atlanta Braves. I turned sixty in December 1997.

130

For forty-eight years, I was the director of the Federal Bureau of Investigation. During my tenure, I built an efficient crime-detection system and attacked organized crime. After World War II, I targeted Communist activities and became controversial because of FBI harassment of left-wing dissenters. After my death in 1972, reports of my unusual personal lifestyle somewhat marred my reputation. The FBI building in Washington, D.C., is named in my honor.

Who Am I?

131 After the Khmer Rouge victory in Cambodia, in 1975, I became the new government's prime minister. Under my regime, an estimated three million Cambodians died from executions, forced labor, and famine. In 1979, an invasion forced me to leave the capital, and I was replaced later that same year as leader of the Khmer Rouge. In 1997 that group sentenced me to house arrest for life. I died the following year.

Who Am I?

132

I was the attorney general of California from 1939 to 1943, and its governor from 1943 to 1953. I became one of the most dynamic chief justices of the Supreme Court, guiding the court in a number of landmark civil-rights decisions, most notably *Brown* v. *Board of Education* in 1954. After the death of President Kennedy, I was chosen to head the commission that investigated his assassination.

Who Am I?

133 Even though my movie roles have required me to be **slapped, beaten, sexually violated, and stabbed, I am currently the idol of millions of teenage girls.** I have portrayed a drug addict, a bisexual poet, a doomed lover who commits suicide, and a mentally retarded boy. For this last part, in *What's Eating Gilbert Grape?* I was nominated for an Oscar. Oh, yes, I have also starred in the biggest box-office hit of all time.

134

I was the great-granddaughter of Henry VII, and was famous for my beauty, piety, and intelligence.

After Edward VI died on July 6, 1553, I reluctantly accepted the crown and was proclaimed queen. Alas, my reign lasted only ten days, after which the lord mayor of London replaced me, proclaiming Mary Tudor queen. I was executed on Tower Green in 1554.

135

Prior to meeting my husband, Juan Perón, I was a dancer, but in 1973 I was elected vice president of Argentina. When Juan died in 1974, I succeeded him to the presidency. In 1976, I was deposed in a military coup and placed under arrest. I was later freed and went into exile in Spain.

Who Am I ?

Q. 134 Lady Jane Grey

136

I was first a patient, then, six years later, a graduate of the Perkins Institute for the Blind.
As Helen Keller's teacher, I pioneered techniques of education for those handicapped by blindness, using a touch-teaching system. During the early 1920s, Helen and I helped to publicize the new American Foundation for the Blind, and lobbied for its program of increased opportunities for the sightless.

137

I was a graduate of the U.S. Military Academy at West Point. I became a U.S. senator from Mississippi and, in 1853, was appointed secretary of war under President Franklin Pierce. I helped establish the Smithsonian Institution, but I am best remembered as president of the Confederate States of America during the Civil War.

A 136 Anne Sullivan Macy

138

I was born in 1503 and became a physician and astrologer. Catherine de Médicis consulted me, and I was physician to Charles IX. It is reputed that I affected remarkable cures during outbreaks of the plague in southern France. My rhymed prophecies, called *Centuries,* gained me the favor of the French court, and throughout the ages my predictions have been subjected to many interpretations.

139

I started my career as a radio journalist, became a television reporter and anchor, and appeared in the movie *The Color Purple*, but am most famous for my TV talk show. Not only am I the most admired woman on television today, I am also the highest paid.

140

Although my reign as pope was relatively short (October 18, 1958–June 3, 1963), I was one of the most progressive and popular popes in the history of the Catholic Church. **My outstanding achievement was the Second Vatican Council, which rejuvenated the church.**

Who Am I ?

141

My daughter sang the national anthem at President Bill Clinton's second inauguration. My son is a newly elected congressman from Chicago, Illinois. I was born into poverty in Greenville, South Carolina, became a Baptist minister in 1968, and was an associate of Martin Luther King Jr. I ran for president as a Democrat in 1984 and 1988 in an effort to increase voter registration and put black issues on the national agenda.

142

I am probably the foremost art figure of the twentieth century.

Although I was born in Spain, I lived most of my ninety-one years in France. My 1907 work *Les Demoiselles d'Avignon* was a significant development in cubism. *Guernica,* another landmark work, was an impassioned condemnation of war and fascism.

143

Branch Rickey signed me to play baseball for the Brooklyn Dodgers in 1945, and in 1947 I shattered a half century tradition of segregation by being the first African-American to play baseball in the major leagues. I became Rookie of the Year, and led the Dodgers to six World Series appearances in the ten years I was with the team. In 1962, I became the first African-American to enter the National Baseball Hall of Fame.

Who Am I?

144 On the night of April 14–15, 1912, the British ocean liner *Titanic* sank on her maiden voyage after striking an iceberg in the North Atlantic. The disaster claimed the lives of more than 1,500 of the 2,200 passengers and crew. I was the captain of the *Titanic,* and had served the vessel's owner, the White Star Line, with a perfect record for twenty-five years. I was scheduled to retire after this ill-fated voyage, but instead went down with my ship.

145

Genius Question: My name was Annie Moore. In 1892, at age fifteen, I left Ireland for America, landing in New York. On my arrival, now an immigrant, I experienced something no one had before but many would. What was it?

Q. 144 Edward J. Smith

146

I am an English king, most famous for my stunning victory over the French at the Battle of Agincourt in 1415, defeating an army eight times larger than mine. William Shakespeare wrote a play about me, which has been brought to film twice, by Laurence Olivier and Kenneth Branagh.

147

On my seventieth birthday, I celebrated with eight hundred of my closest friends, spending $2 million for the party. I loved motorcycles, toy boats, and toy soldiers, but my most famous collection was of twelve Fabergé eggs. When I was sixty, I became the first balloonist to cross the country, and I did so in twenty-one days. I was even a two-time state senator. With all these extracurricular activities, I was still able to transform the first business publication in the nation, started by my father, into one of the most successful magazines in America.

Who Am I ?

148 I am one of America's premier feminists and journalists. I was a founding editor of both *New York* magazine and *Ms.* magazine. I became a spokesperson for many feminist causes, and helped organize the Women's Political Caucus in 1971. My most recent book is *Moving beyond Words* (1994).

Who Am I?

149

Born in Ireland and educated in Germany, I became the principal cellist at the Stuttgart Court Opera. However, my fame as a composer overshadowed my other musical abilities once I moved to America. My forty operettas include such favorites as *Babes in Toyland*, *The Red Mill*, and *Naughty Marietta*. Already a rich man, I helped fashion American musical copyright law and was a founder of ASCAP (American Society of Composers, Authors, and Publishers), which protects artists' rights. I died in 1924.

150

Genius Question: My name is Samuel Wilson of Troy, New York. I was born in 1766 and died eighty-eight years later. During the War of 1812, I was an inspector of army supplies, and after the war I returned to my civilian job as a meat packer. Even though I never served in the armed forces, I am the foremost symbol of patriotism in the United States. What am I called?

Who Am I?